DIPPING
INTO
ADVENT
REFLECTIONS FOR
ADVENT & CHRISTMAS

ALAN HILLIARD

Published by Messenger Publications, 2019

ISBN 978 1 78812 089 0
Copyright © Alan Hilliard, 2019
All photographs copyright © Alan Hilliard, 2019

Designed by Messenger Publications Design Department
Typeset in Gill Sans, Didot, Rockwell & Dancing Script
Printed by Hussar Books

Messenger Publications,
37 Lower Leeson Street, Dublin D02 W938
www.messenger.ie

Contents

Introduction

The world is changing, changing by the day and even by the hour. Sometimes change is good but other times it can leave us quite dizzy. The solid structures of the past, whether they supported us or may have concealed things that caused hurt and pain, are weakening. We are moving away, as a society, from a faith supported by hierarchy and structure.

This book reflects on that shift. Advent and Christmas no longer define us in the way they did. Some of us have held on to the spirit of these seasons, but in Ireland more generally we have lost the plot. Advent and Christmas have been stolen by the market, and rather than be guided by a thoughtful, religious sensibility during what is a time of wonder we are guided by the not-so-subtle drumbeat of the market. Happiness via consumerism: Black Fridays and January sales have pushed the infant from the crib.

The reflections in this book challenge you to dip into the real spirit of the season. You may like some and not others, and this may change day-to-day.

Feedback from my last book Dipping into Lent simply said 'more of the same please!' Thank you one and all for your encouragement. I hope that this book helps you hold on to your sense of the world in a time of great change, and to resist the seductive influences of a consumerism.

It is my sincere hope that in reading this book you may feel a little closer to the God who loves us and gave of himself for us. Pope Francis has said that we now live not in an era of change but in the change of an era. If this is the case we have to find a spirituality to suit the era we live in.

Mam and Dad on a Summer's Day

Dedication

This book is dedicated to my mother who passed away while this book was being written. I miss her every day though I know she is with me. I continue to be inspired by her gentle soul and I continue to laugh with her every day. She saw the craziness of the world and she helped me see it too. She saw beyond it all too which helped her to live and die well.

This book is also dedicated to a lady who lived on the road I grew up on. Mary Dunne passed away five months after my mother. She was a great support to me over the years of mam's illnesses. They lived on the same road, they are buried in the same row of graves and now they are partakers in the same choir!

#a_pint

We were sitting over our pints talking. Two priests catching up. We were beyond the usual gossip and stuff that is talked about by priests.

'How did the (Christmas) ceremonies go?' I asked. 'Grand', he said. 'What did you talk about at the Midnight Mass?' 'Nothing much,' he said 'told a story'. 'Was it any good?', I asked curiously. 'Well they stayed quiet for it which is good I suppose.'

He went on, 'Do you remember during the summer the sparrow that got into my house, and it kept flying into the windows trying to get out? Well I told them that story. I remember that poor bird kept flying away from me and I only wanted to help it.' He sipped his pint. 'It was as frustrating as hell; here was me trying to help and it kept flying in the opposite direction.' Pausing for a moment he said, 'I suppose if I was that bird looking at me there's enough to be frightened about'. I nodded in agreement and noticed a slight look of rebuke from him.

'A thought flashed through my mind as I tried to entice the winged creature out of an open window … I thought to myself if I could just be like the bird for one minute I could get its trust and lead it to a safe place'. He stopped, staying silent for quite a while. I grew impatient. 'And?' I said rather inquisitively. 'And what?' he asked. 'And what was the rest of the story?' my raised voice caused a few to turn their heads. 'There is no rest of the story,' and, pausing for a moment, he took another sip and put the pint down squarely on the beer mat 'I just said "you know God became like us so that we could become like him"'.

That line kept playing over and over again in my head for weeks. Aren't I the silly sparrow!

'I'm perpetually in limbo. Maybe I want too many things at once and nothing passionately enough.'

Elif Shafak

Three Daughters of Eve, (London: Penguin Random House, 2016), p. 86.

#ageing

When the Irish Sisters of Charity arrived in Sydney, Australia one of their main works was to be with the dying. Many people there were in need due to deportation or migration, and were without families, but the sisters committed to those who were at the end of their days promising them that they would not die alone. They sat, prayed, mopped brows and conversed with those who were approaching life's end.

In his book *The Loneliness of the Dying* the sociologist Norbert Elias wrote that 'never before have people died as noiselessly and hygienically as today in these societies [societies of the Global North], and never in social conditions so much fostering solitude'. The contrast between the Global North and Global South is stark. The moral fibre of these two economic regions, one poor and the other wealthy, is revealed in way they treat those who are elderly and dying.

The Gospel of Luke presents two characters in the early days of Jesus who are elderly. Simeon and Anna both 'hang around' the Temple. Neither have lost their sense of purpose and mission despite their age. They have a reason to live and the Temple is a place where that reason finds nurturing. Both recognised the child who was to be the fulfilment of the promise of God, and both rejoiced in that moment of encounter when Joseph and Mary brought Jesus to the Temple.

Simeon's prayer is so powerful that it is said every night in the Night Prayer of the Church. It is recited by hundreds of thousands of people who pray on their own or who pray in community. Let us not lock up those who are elderly in unnecessary isolation. They have great lessons to teach us, amazing wisdom with which to nourish us and unstinting insight that can provoke us into appreciating the precious gift of life.

'At last, all powerful master, you give leave to your servant to go in peace, according to your promise. For my eyes have seen your salvation which you have prepared for all nations, the light to enlighten the Gentiles and give glory to Israel, your people.'

The Prayer of Simeon (Lk 2:29–32)

#agnostic

'I'm an agnostic anyway', he said. This ploy is used by many who get into a life situation that requires a little bit of drilling down; it's a reaction to change or even an attempt to get off the subject. I wasn't going to let him away that easy.

'On a scale of one to ten, ten being good, how good an agnostic are you?' I asked rather mischievously. There was a painful pause as he was trying very hard to comprehend my question. 'Do you know what an agnostic is?' I offered. It was like I'd released a safety valve. He visibly relaxed and said, in his defence, 'I'm not sure really, I think it's that you don't know whether, or what or who to believe or not!' 'Well then,' I said, 'where are you on the one to ten scale?' He held his head back and let out a guffaw. 'Tell me a bit more … I think I need to brush up on my agnosticism … ironic that it's a Catholic priest who is helping me understand it a bit better!'

'To begin with' I said, 'agnosticism is not a belief'. He looked at me quite puzzled, 'Oh yes,' I continued 'people talk about it as if it's a belief system but in actual fact it's a methodology only. A methodology is a process that we put in place to help us understand things better'.

He seemed more interested. I told him that a guy called Thomas Henry Huxley coined the term 'agnosticism' in the 1860s. He argued that only those beliefs that could be shown to be true counted as knowledge, and so had value. However he did admit that we could not be certain about whether God existed or not, so I could surmise then that like religion agnosticism is not a perfect system!

'He didn't really have a problem with 'not knowing' because he saw this as a precursor to knowing,' I said, thinking out loud 'he was just very intense about the methodology that was employed to prove something'. Then I served the killer left hook, 'In fairness to

Huxley, agnosticism was never supposed to be used as a copout or a lazy person's approach to religious belief; it demanded rigour and application and answers'.

There was silence for a while; 'I don't think I'm even near a one on the scale' he said rather despondently. 'Take heart,' I said, 'there is a starting point if you are interested'. 'Go on', he replied rather enthusiastically. 'Huxley was of the view that while he saw no reason for believing in religion, especially Christianity, he admitted to having no means of disproving it'. 'I'm listening', he said. 'Do you mind if we have a chat about those bits of Christianity that you can't disprove or would that be an offense to your agnosticism?' We talked late into the night and it was great.

> 'Steer (Professor M.D.) claimed the typical frequency at which anger was expressed was 220 vibrations per second. Hitler's voice clocked in at 228 vibrations. This relentless shrill pitch dazed audiences 'in much the same way as we are stunned by a car horn' ...
> If, as the monks believe, we seal our lips in order to draw closer to a higher truth, we shout to acquire earthly clout.'
>
> George Prochnik

In Pursuit of Silence; Listening for Meaning in a Noisy World,
(New York: Anchor Books, 2010), pp. 67-70.

#articifical_intelligence

There was a time when AI was an agricultural term, now it is a one that tries to describe what awaits us as computers take on the tasks that humans once did. The scope and range of AI is both awesome and worrying. There is much speculation as to what computers will do for us and how they will affect employment and unemployment, and there is growing discussion and speculation on the ethic behind the machines ... if there is any that is!

The self-driving car is a topic that is attracting a lot of investment and discussion, but it also raises many ethical issues. A study in 2015 revealed that most people thought that an out-of-control car should be programmed to prioritise pedestrians over the driver. However when asked would they buy a car that was programmed to protect the greater good at the expense of the driver they said no!

This example shows us that while we may have great intentions for humanity and we can espouse altruism, at the end of the day our actions are quite the opposite. As someone said to me recently when they were describing the new people moving into their area; 'they think everyone's dog should be on a lead except theirs'.

'Only by being a man or woman for others
does one become fully human.'

Pedro Arrupe SJ

. . . .

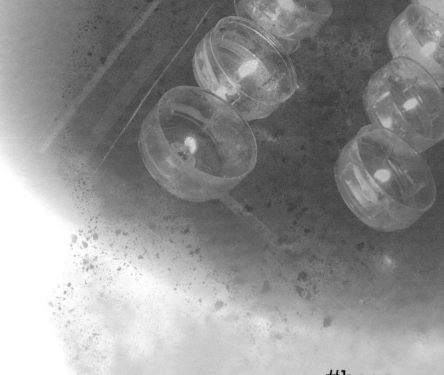

#bags

It was Christmas Eve. The buses were packed as everyone clambered on with last minute shopping. I don't know how she managed to pay her fare; she had so many bags hanging from her hands, arms and shoulders. She plonked the entire collection in the luggage area at the entrance to the bus, and you could she her relief as she visibly enjoyed the feeling of blood rushing though her hands, arms and shoulders once again.

She got off at the same stop as me. The busyness of the bus was drowned out by her cry 'My bags … they're gone!' Someone had taken her last minute shopping. Presents from Santa, gifts for under the Christmas tree, kindly items for neighbours, clothes for the day and the necessary ingredients to enhance the dinner … all gone.

The financial cost was huge but what upset her most was trying to think of what she was going to say to some of the people she'd bought gifts for, especially her children. She could see their disappointed faces and she was stumped as how she could begin

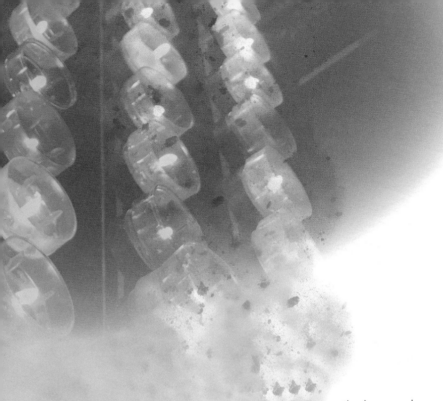

to explain what had happened. Someone just got on the bus, eyed the bags and got off with them at an earlier stop. Christmas Eve – the season of goodwill drained away before our eyes.

There is no doubt that the world can challenge our efforts at goodwill. At times it might appear to us that trying to make the world better place is akin to pushing a rock up a steep hill, but the Christian cannot give into despair. The God we believe in would never have joined us on our dusty roads if he didn't believe in the triumph of the good. If despair was king, hope would never have been born among us in human flesh .

> 'I've decided to stick with love.
> Hate is too great a burden to bear.'
>
> Martin Luther King Jr

#bucket_list

'God be with the days when the funeral used to be about the person who died' she said despairingly as she threw her wet umbrella into the corner of the room. 'What in God's name are you on about now?' I asked her, not having a clue what she was on about. 'I would have been home before the rain only some 'wan' got up after the funeral and went on and on about granny…sure she hardly ever went to see her…and do you know what?... all she said was how great she was herself …said nothing about the poor lady who died…and God knows there was a lot to say…she was a great woman'.

  'She went on and on about her bucket list for her gran and all that they should have done…that woman spent her life carrying buckets for other people.' She never cursed much but she was flying now as she went on … 'when I die say your prayers and put me in the hole in the ground…I don't want any of that auld nonsense…they'd be fit to say their prayers'. She concluded with that familiar impish grin. 'You know the final hymn was *How Great Thou Art*…I think your 'wan' who spoke thought it was for her'.

The idea of Paradise as the future home of the Blessed is replaced by the concept of self-fulfilment in the here and now.

Ulrich Beck

· · · · · · · · ·

A God of One's Own, (Cambridge, Polity Press, 2010), pp. 129.

#burnt_out

'Are you looking forward to Christmas?' I asked for the sake of conversation. 'Looking forward … looking forward … looking forward' she replied with increasing decibels each time. I felt if she said it one more time she'd explode! I didn't know or couldn't guess what she was going to say next. 'I'm burnt out on Christmas already and it's only the beginning of December. I'm listening to Christmas Carols since Halloween and one window I saw back then had witches on one side and Santa on the other … looking forward … I wish I was'.

When she saw me laugh she settled a bit and said, 'I'm burnt out on the whole thing without ever having been on fire about it … if you don't take hold of the real message for yourself then others will make sure that what they want the season to be will grab you and never let go'.

'Monsters exist, but they are too few in number to be truly dangerous. More dangerous are the common men, the functionaries ready to believe and to act without asking questions.'

Primo Levi

Primo Levi in Rutagengwa (ed.), *Love Prevails: One Couple's Story of Faith and Survival in the Rwandan Genocide*, (New York: Orbis Books, 2019), p. 152.

#coffee

It's a place I go to regularly for a coffee. It was the beginning of November, All Soul's Day to be exact. I told the cashier, 'I love your Halloween costume'. She looked at me funny and said, in her eastern-European accent, 'This is not my Halloween costume – this is our Christmas uniform!' I was quite shocked and sure enough when I looked more closely there was a reindeer on her jumper smiling back at me, and she had antlers clipped onto her head. Seeing my shock she said, 'yes, in my country we would not do this until much later,' rubbing her thumb and two fore-fingers together she said, 'but here it is all about money'.

> *'What they all have in common [the Gods of Egypt] is that they are confiscatory gods who demand endless produce and who authorise endless systems of production that are, in principle, insatiable.'*

Walter Brueggemann

. . . .

Sabbath as Resistance: Saying No to the Culture of Now,
(Kentucky: Westminster John Knox Press, 2014), p. 2.

#culture

I always found Christmas in Bondi, Australia a strange experience. Don't get me wrong it was a great experience: the sunshine, the young people packing the Church, the camaraderie and the ability to create family environments among friends and strangers. It was not a day for the beach as it was too busy, too hot and a little crazy. So why did I find it strange? I think it's more to do with what I am used to. The cultural wrapping in the northern hemisphere was slightly different than that in the southern hemisphere. Up north we huddle in from the cold while down south they crank up the air-conditioner. In the north we light fires while down south they are scared of fires at this time of year, as bush-fires can lead to death and disaster. There are many other differences.

Regardless of the historical setting all faith requires a culture in order to exist or thrive. If it tries to exist outside of a culture in a pure form then you have a foundation for fundamentalism. Even Jesus chose a culture in which he could dwell and through it he allowed us to ponder the mystery of the Father's love for the world. Over time, however, the culture can become over identified with the religious content and the religious content can be squeezed out, and we are left with a confusion accompanied with hollow and empty rituals. In short we are left with the wrapping paper and no gift!

'The debate about inculturation relies on a simple principle: religion is not culture, but it cannot exist outside culture.'

Olivier Roy

· · · · · · · · · ·

Holy Ignorance; When Religion and Culture Part Ways,
(London: C. Hurst&Co. Ltd., 2010), p. 62.

#dreamer

Oftentimes the term 'dreamer' is used to describe someone who is out of touch with reality. They've more or less got their heads in the clouds. St Joseph was a dreamer who dealt with reality. His dreams were the key to the safety and security of those he loved. He didn't appear to argue with his dreams, rather he trusted them. It's very hard to interpret dreams yet some make a profession of it. I once read an article by Carl Jung that spoke about the time he spent with Sigmund Freud when they tried to interpret one another's dreams. Jung didn't agree with Freud's view of dreams which leaves little hope for me to work out what they are about!

I believe dreams are sent by God not to frighten us but to heal us. Sometimes issues like grief run deep in us and we cannot process them with the brain alone. The deep unconscious, spiritual dimension of our being cares for our soul as the brain is ill equipped to deal with everything that comes our way.

> 'Westerners don't naturally understand the inner world... The Western Church really isn't that spiritual. It doesn't understand spirituality. Buying and selling in the temple makes more sense to us.'

Richard Rohr

• • • • • • • • •

Radical Grace, (Cincinnati: St Anthony Messenger Press, 1993), p. 87.

23

#drink

She was always larger than life and didn't think before she spoke. It got her into trouble more times than you can imagine. This time though it was different. The diagnosis was bad and whether she knew or didn't know didn't matter because she was still her 'larger than life' self.

Reflecting on her life and loves, she spoke of her husband who was known to be a heavy drinker and often missing when she needed a husband and the children needed a father. Whatever was going on for him at the time he chose the path of 'self medication' to put his troubles at a distance from his mind.

'Father', she started, 'I was better off when he was drinking'. 'How come?' I asked in a puzzled tone. 'Well father ... when he was on the drink he was out from under my feet'. She paused for effect. She may never have been on the boards of the national theatre but her timing was perfection. 'Since he's gone off the drink he's doing nothing but going down to the Church, chewing statues and coming home spouting chalk!'

'Without wonder, the world of men turns into compulsive activity and self-sealing systems of thought and social organisation, and men, at best, become experts and efficient professionals and, at worst, puppets and functionaries of assorted institutions.'

Sam Keen

. . . .

Fire in the Belly: On Being a Man, (London: Judy Piaktus Ltd., 1992), p. 155.

#faces

Herod is an ever-present character in the Christmas story. He appears when there is change of direction and that direction is not usually a good one for others. Usually the other characters have to flee and hide to protect themselves when Herod rears his head.

But who was Herod and what was going on for him? The Romans usually picked someone from the locality to run things for them. The world then had no centres of power. These days, aided by technology, centres of powers can be identified and can claim to represent the wider community. These centres are the heart of attack, negotiation and settlement. In the days when the Jesus was born things were different. Power was more localised; centres of power were mostly based on trade, but to run a country or region effectively you had to put someone in place who knew the locality. A stranger would never get on top of the situation. There was no covert or even satellite surveillance then; everything was known by observation and conversation.

Herod had a divided loyalty. He was known by his own and he was answerable to Rome. He was responsible for everything that happened in that region and if his chain of command was not pleased with the way he did things they could find him a new role. We may ask who was Herod? But I'm sure he asked himself the same question.

One pressure that often comes up at Christmas is that people have to become somebody or be somebody they are not; a bit like Herod. Situations in families and life generally can make us put on a face that is not our real or truest self. If this is done over time it can be quite damaging. If a child does it in order to survive a toxic family setting, they can end up as a very mixed up person in adulthood.

While Herod grew in different directions trying to protect his status and pandering to those who paid him, we are told that Jesus grew in wisdom, age and stature. He was aided by the fact that the only person he had to be was himself. This is what attracts many people to Christianity today – the integrity and authenticity of the man Jesus. He could be himself; he didn't have to put on a face and he didn't seem to worry about impressing people. Take it or leave it was his approach. Unlike others who inspire world faiths, and even the Christian faith, nowhere did Jesus need to undergo 'a conversion'. He is on a continuum – what you see is what you get … all the time, and that continuum continues in our time too!

'There is never any suggestion of Christ having undergone a conversion experience. All the Gospels affirm his presence and his understanding as something that just was.'

James Alison

The Joy of Being Wrong. (New York: Crossroad Publishing Company, 1998), p. 26.

#flight_into_egypt

Look closely at the picture. You can see a man reaching out of the boat and a mother with her new-born baby at the other end of the boat. The action of reaching into the water to rescue the drowning person puts those in the boat at risk. Both the man and the woman, even though she holds the child, have their arms and hands open as they gesture towards the water. They aren't holding back in fear; they are actively engaged in assisting the person who is struggling in the water.

This boat is a depiction of the Holy Family on their journey to Egypt and is found in many sea-faring homes. This particular moulding was given as a gift to Pope Francis when he visited the

island of Lampedusa on his first trip as Pontiff in 2013. When he saw it he said that there was only one place for this important message and that was in Lampedusa. It can now be found in a display case in the little church on the island for all to see.

No longer does the law of the sea necessarily protect those in need – it protects those in power. Law no longer bestows 'natural' rights for every human being but now creates zones where rights don't exist, so we can turn a blind eye to those in need and sedate our consciences. Our basic Christian instinct to reach out is now curtailed by law and political correctness.

This is the new emerging 'world order'. The Christmas message has subsequently become more relevant and holds a more profound challenge for all who claim the name Christian. Like the family in the boat we might experience more risk and fear when we reach out to others but this is our true calling and is how we participate in the redemptive power of our God. Let us now try to correct the direction that our world is taking and try to steer it towards calmer, safer waters where safety is both guaranteed as a natural and divine order, and not just a benefit to those in bigger boats.

'In Fr Daniel Groody's words, Jesus is the quintessential migrant. God migrated from heaven to earth, taking on our humanity, and died on the cross in order to return us from exile to our true home.'

Deirdre Cornell

• • • • • • • • •

Jesus was a Migrant, (New York: Orbis Books, 2014), pp. 25–26.

#for_cribs_sake

I wonder what possessed St Francis during Christmas in 1223 when he grabbed a few animals, including an ox and an ass, to recreate the nativity scene at Bethlehem? Why was it that, in this little Italian town of Greccio, nestled into the hills and lying approximately one hundred kilometres north of Rome, he decided to recreate that scene?

A sensible person might have suggested that he should have just gone to the local church, said a prayer, maybe light a candle and just get on with things but he didn't. Seemingly his style was that of 'dramatic gesture', which was usually theatrical and provocative. To his credit, all these years later we still resort to the image he recreated then. If his life wasn't given over to God he certainly would have had a future in the marketing division of whatever companies were around in those days!

I wonder then why he just didn't go to a church and say a prayer? Maybe he felt he couldn't recognise the God he knew there. That era celebrated the divinity of God. It relied heavily on depictions of the resurrection and transformation of the Risen Lord displayed in an iconic-like way. These icons told of the victory won to rescue a sinful humanity from its fallen state.

Francis found among the people he served (who were mostly poor and neglected) that they had a great sense of their sinfulness and little sense of the joy that comes from knowing the Father's love for us. Those he lived among and served may have been close to believing that they deserved their state because of their sinfulness. Francis knew that those who had wealth hadn't got their wealth because they were free from sin; he had seen this firsthand in his own family! He also had a great sense that those who were cast aside were cast aside by fellow human beings, not by a punishing vengeful God.

The crib may have been an attempt by Francis to say let's begin again and get a perspective on this story that has become unbalanced in its artistic presentation. His God was born into vulnerability and uncertainty, like most of the world's population, his crib was a living representation of this fact. Yes Jesus was exalted but he was also humbled and he had humble beginnings. His Father and our Father was with him through it all. Quite simply Easter wasn't the beginning for Francis, Christmas was.

> *'Start by doing what's necessary,*
> *then do what's possible; and suddenly*
> *you are doing the impossible.'*
>
> St Francis
>
> · · · · · · · · · ·

#gobbeldygook

It wasn't the most pleasant job I have ever done. The toilet was blocked, and I had to call on the services of a plumber. Time was ticking on and it was getting close to one in the morning. In this most humble setting, we got to the subject of religion and belief and of course the upcoming events of Christmas.

'I have my own faith', he said, 'I don't feel I have to go to the Church like … but I go like, me and God have it worked out between ourselves' as he pointed to his chest. He did a bit more plunging as he struggled to remove the blockage. 'I feel sorry for the young ones today … they've nothing … there's nothing steering the ship like … ', he paused to take a breath. 'I've tried to tell my lad about how it's important but do you know what he said?' He waited for an answer from me, 'No', I said. 'Gobbledygook … that's what he said it is … all gobbledygook'.

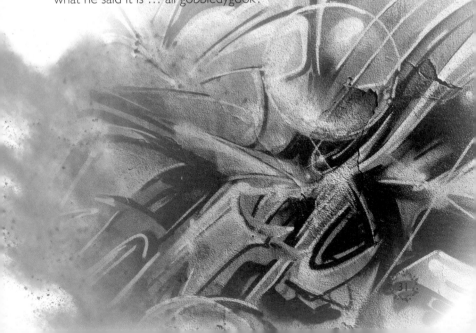

31

He was evidently more agitated and was plunging with more deliberate force. Next minute there was a strange rush of water and an almighty gurgling. 'There you are now, blockage removed!' Leaning on his plunger he said, 'I've seen a lot in life, and I know gobbledygook when I see it'. He was more animated and he was thumping his chest at this stage as he said, 'this isn't gobbledygook; I know what I believe. It's got me through enough scrapes'. For once I was grateful for gobbledygook, not that I profess faith in it, but it gave him that little bit of extra fight that allowed him to clear the pipe and allowed me to get to my bed.

'Billions pray to God, "oh give me victory, give me money, give me a Ferrari, do-this-do-that ..." but hardly anyone goes to the trouble of getting to know Him.'

Elif Shafak

. . . .

Three Daughters of Eve, (London: Penguin Random House, 2014), p. 38.

#going_like_blazes

She was sitting in the pew beside him. They were a young couple. One could presume they were married from the rings on their fingers. From the time the Mass started her leg was going like blazes. It wouldn't stay still. It seemed like all the nervous energy of her life was concentrated in her right leg and it just kept hopping up and down.

Funnily enough the opening prayer of the Mass for the Advent liturgy urged us to 'resolve to run forth'... she looked like she was going to 'run forth' out of the pew any time and break the land speed record!

At one stage during the Mass she put her head on his shoulder. He tried to shrug her away but she put her head back. He pecked her on the forehead. It was a gentle kiss and for a few moments the leg stopped.

I once heard someone say that the coming of Jesus to the world was akin to the Father kissing us. An intimate expression of his love, care and concern for us and the promise that he can do more and we can do more together. It's a love like this that gets our legs going like blazes in the right direction.

> *'I felt its presence without the usual barricades of 'me-ness' or 'you-ness' ... I am compelled to believe that, I, like many others, have underestimated this mystical, spiritual dimension.'*

Howard Kirschenbaum and Valerie Land Henderson

· · · · · · · · · ·

(Eds), *The Carl Rogers Reader,* (London: Constable and Company Ltd., 1990), p. 138.

#greed

There are many books, articles and programs that cover the causes and sources of the last recession. They speculate, manipulate, ponder and decide. Blame is apportioned and advice is given, but we can never turn back the clock and start over again. Hindsight is, as someone once said, an exact science.

I read a lot about the crash and events that led up to it. Between banks, governments, boards and regulatory bodies there are plenty of institutions that we can get justifiably angry with. One article I read dealt out a fair share of blame, however there was one line

in it that burnt itself into my mind. To paraphrase the sentence it basically said 'no one can legislate for greed'. Many financial institutions overstepped what one would consider their ethical limits. However, how many people, aided by a lack of oversight by many organisations, simply lost the run of themselves? How many people put pressure on their own banks and lending institutions to extend their credit or else they'd take their custom elsewhere? Sometimes we get the institutions we deserve.

I was told a story about a victim of the crash who was travelling on a bus. He got one of those phone calls to confirm that he was in trouble and that his former assets were now lead boots dragging him further and further into the mire of debt and insolvency. He was rather curt with the person at the other end of the phone and as he hung up rather angrily an elderly lady who was seated behind him leaned forward and tapped him on the shoulder. He turned around and the lady spoke in rather consoling tones, 'God love you son; is it your first recession?'

Advent is time to decide my approach to greed. This is not our first Christmas – it can be different this year.

> `We now have a global overclass which makes
> all the major economic decisions, and makes
> them in entire independence of the legislatures,
> and a fortiori of the will of the voters,
> of any given country.`
>
> Richard Rorty
>
> • • • • • • • • • •
>
> *Philosophy and Social Hope*, (London: Penguin, 1999), p. 233.

#hope

The *Hôtel des Mille Collines* was an unusual place to be in the run up to Christmas. I was staying in the hotel made famous when over a thousand people took refuge there during the Rwandan Genocide.

It is quite a comfortable place and structurally it is the same as it was in 1994. I travelled up and down the country meeting survivors of the genocide with a group of researchers from Notre

Dame University, stopping a various sites where the worst atrocities occurred. Having left Dublin City, which was alive with Christmas lights and decorations, I noted the seeming absence of decorations in Rwanda. I spotted only two, one in the hotel lobby and one other in a small shopping centre across the road from the hotel.

It was the season of Advent and as the days passed, and as I listened to stories of the horror of the genocide, I began to articulate deep questions about life and about Christian life in particular. We speak about hope in Advent, I thought, but how can you have hope when there is nothing left to hope for? I asked one religious sister, who had witnessed the murder of her students, this question. She talked about the awful silence that dwelt over the land as people waited for death, torture and decimation.

She said to me, 'when you see evil, taste evil, look into the eye of evil you have no choice but to go in the other direction'. I realised in that moment I had an academic relationship with evil. It was something I pondered and moved on from, but I knew from the

way she spoke that her experience of evil was much more than academic interest. 'When you experience this type of evil and when you reflect on it you have no choice but to walk towards the good – that is the only hope you have otherwise you get consumed by the evil that surrounds you. It is not even a choice you just cannot not do it'. She paused, 'The purpose of my life is solely to place goodness on the throne of God each and every day that I live'.

What a lady … real Christmas doesn't need decorations!

*'Genuine hope is not blind optimism.
It is hope with open eyes, which sees the
suffering yet believes in the future.'*

Juergen Moltmann

#in_unison

City-centre parishes are full of interesting people. At Sunday Mass young and old gather to say goodbye to the weekend or hello to the week ahead. The priest was very competent. He said a gracious Mass and the homily left me with something to think about; at least I felt closer to God as a result of being there.

He introduced the Our Father as the prayer that unites us as a Christian people. Be it richly symbolical or just plain funny the congregation were far from united: I counted about six different paces at which the prayer was recited. The priest with the aid of his microphone was the one to follow so to speak. There was a group of elderly ladies at the front who may have been members of the same prayer group but they were doing their best to slow him down into a slow meditative and meaningful rendition of the prayer, where every word was sacred and vacuum packed! There was a man in front of me who kept fiddling with his hearing aid during Mass anyway, so he was just doing his own thing. From his frustration it appeared as if his batteries had packed in. I remained silent as I listened to the various recitations and was particularly distracted by the mother and daughter behind me who were trying to get to the finish line first. They finished, the man in front of me with the dead hearing aid came in next, then the priest, and then the pious prayer group up the front came in late well behind the rest.

I wonder did the shepherds have this problem. I wonder when they uttered the Hosannas were their minds on different things or where they truly enraptured by the child to the extent that they uttered their song of praise in unison. Or when they went home 'glorying and praising God for all they had heard and seen' were they of one mind and heart?

It's consoling to think that the followers of Jesus were of one heart and mind at a various occasions in the evolution of the Church. However I suppose it is even more consoling to know we can go at our own pace when the occasion demands it!

'It is never Christ who is absent or far away from us, it is we who are distracted, far off or indifferent. Christ's existence is independent of us, he is not confined to the subjective feelings we may or may not have of him.'

Brother Roger of Taizé

. . . .

A Life We never Dared Hope For, (Mowbray, 1980), p. 49.

#knots

It is less and less the case now, but as a child one of the most frustrating jobs was the Christmas tree lights. Today lights are cheaper and hence disposable but year in and year out we had the same lights. The tree would be up, decorations would be laid out ready to go on the tree and then there were the lights!

No matter how carefully you packed the lights the year before they'd always end up in knots and so the task of untying began. Unravelling the wire would have been easy if it wasn't for the cumbersome task of pulling lights through the various loops of wire. Mentally one had to identify the beginning, the middle and the end of the lights and decide which direction to go in order to get an unknotted line of lights laid out across the room before it was wrapped around the tree. Hours later one looked with satisfaction at the length of wire stretched across the floor with the various coloured bulbs, cribs, or Santa's heads made of glass that covered the light bulbs and gave them their characteristic colourful glow.

The trouble only started at this stage, however, as they were yet to be plugged in and yes inevitably the worst happened – nothing would light up or at best only half of them would. The painful process of finding spare bulbs. This often necessitated a trip into town to an electrical shop for overpriced bulbs. (And let me put in on the record here before we ever developed a policy of recycling nothing was ever thrown out and nothing was ever replaced unless it had totally fallen apart!) Each of the fifty bulbs along the length of wire would have to be replaced in a slow logical fashion in order to find out which bulbs were causing the break in the electrical current. At times it felt like Christmas would be well over before we'd have light on the tree.

When Pope Francis left Ireland after his first visit while on sabbatical in Milltown in 1979 he went on to visit Germany. While he was there he came across a Baroque painting entitled *Wallfahrtsbild* by the artist Johann Georg Melchior Schmidtner (1625–1707) completed in 1700. It is displayed in the Church of St Peter am Perlach in Augsburg, Bavaria. This painting depicts the Blessed Virgin Mary undoing, not Christmas tree lights, but a cord which is full of knots. The painting was donated to the Church by a priest in thanksgiving for a reconciliation that occurred between his grandparents whose marriage had been in difficulty. Working with the counsel of a Jesuit priest they made peace. The priest sat with them for many hours and he prayed on their behalf to the image of our Lady depicted in the painting. His prayer was that Mary would 'untie all knots and smoothen them'.

Untying any knots, be they in life or on the Christmas tree lights, is not easy. If we have any knots may they be given to Mary, who prays with us, maybe in silence, as we just sit with her. Apart from the pains of child-bearing and child-birth I'm sure Mary carried lots of knots in her being that she had to undo. Knots of anxiety and frustration can really mess us up. May we give them to her that she may untie and smoothen them, and so we can unfold a future for ourselves.

`It is not speaking that breaks our silence, but the anxiety to be heard. The words of the proud person impose silence on all others, so that they alone may be heard. The humble person speaks only in order to be spoken to. The humble person asks nothing but an alms, then waits and listens.`

Thomas Merton

. . . .

The Essential Writings, (Bochen, 2001)

#magnifying_glass

Christmas can be like a magnifying glass. When life is good, then things are great and when things are not so good, then life can take on awful proportions. It is as if the situations of life are magnified at Christmas due to the level of expectation we have around the feast.

Of course it'd be wonderful for everyone to have a peaceful, fun-filled celebration, but if that was to happen some of us would have to be very good actors. We can't avoid what's real. One Christmas morning I went out to celebrate Mass. It was a small church and with a quick scan I absorbed who was and wasn't there that morning. I had my homily ready but I had to rethink it immediately.

On my right, as I looked down from the altar, sat a young couple with the cutest new born baby in their arms. Both parents were besotted and proud. They were delighted with the number of people who came up to congratulate them, and they indulged themselves in the good wishes of so many. On my left sat a couple who only three days beforehand had gone through the pain of the loss of their baby as a result of a miscarriage. They were a little older than most couples and not only were they ravaged by the loss, but they wondered if they could ever, ever conceive and have a child again. One couple looked out to seek the congratulations of the assembled, the other looked down, afraid that others would see the pain and sadness which they couldn't hide. It would have been easier not to come to church that Christmas morning.

I don't know what I said that morning, but it didn't refer to either situation as I couldn't ignore the joy of one and the torment of the other. When it came to the sign of peace I paused for a moment and said 'you know we often use the sign of peace to say hello to someone or share a comment or two'. There were a lot of people in the church at that stage and it was slightly uncomfortable as the air was humid. I continued, 'sometimes I feel like a hypocrite offering the sign of peace because there is someone in the church that I don't get on with and yes there may even be someone I can't stand but such is life … I am not as Christian as I'd like to be'. Another pause from me, 'I often see the sign of peace, especially at Christmas, not as an offering of peace but a hope that peace is possible where there presently may be little or no peace … Let us offer one another a sign of Christ's peace'. I noticed the couple on my left hug for quite a few moments and I made sure to offer them my peace; both clasped my hand tightly. About sixteen months later I baptised their newborn child.

This year, no matter what the magnifying glass throws up please pray for the peace that is possible for you or for someone else – 'The Peace of Christ be with you'.

'In our distressed, broken world prayer is truly 'the bond of peace.'

Pierre-François de Béthune OSB

By Faith and Hospitality, (Herefordshire: Gracewing, 2002), p. 53.

#mam_is_dead

It's the last thing I expected to hear three days before Christmas Day, at eight thirty in the morning. 'Mam is dead the firebrigade is with her now.' These were the words of my brother to me from the other end of the phone. The thoughts of what had to be bought, cooked, wrapped or delivered evaporated. The ritual watery shaves and teeth-brushing weren't even contemplated as I made my way to my car. Thankfully it was a Saturday and the roads were clear.

Arriving to the house and bounding up the stairs I found what was relayed to me on the phone to be true. Her words that I had heard many, many times from her wise lips echoed around the room –'death is very final son'. And so it is.

There was also an uncanny deep sense of God's presence in those moments. There was heartbreak and that awful cold silence of death, but God was present. God had come to visit my mother and this time he had taken her with him. Yes it was Christmas and yes it was not the perfect time to lose one's mother but God had spoken. She listened, heard and responded as she always did. This was Annunciation, Visitation and Incarnation run into one swift second. It was the entire mystery of Christmas on display before me but in a most jagged and heart-rending way. We spread events over the table of time; but for God it is but one and the same moment. We cannot begin to get inside this thinking as we are but human in being, nature and understanding. Yet, Christmas tells us that he became like each one of us so that we in turn can become like him in the self-same being, nature and understanding.

Mam's death was the Christmas mystery that lies beyond tinsel and lights but lives in carols, Bible and liturgy. This was and is Christmas in its most wonderful manifestation despite its dreadful hurt and inconvenience.

> 'Happiness does not reside in the absence
> of troubles, but in facing up to them, fighting
> and overcoming them. How different this
> message is from today's almost universal cult
> of bodily and spiritual comfort ...'

Zygmunt Bauman and Stanislaw Obirek

• • • • • • • • • •

On the World and Ourselves, (Cambridge: Polity Press, 2015), p. 20.

#none_greater_than_me

Being squashed in a crowd was an awful thing as a child. I can remember the uneasy feeling of hot air complicated by the fact that I was only five years of age and my view was limited to the lower half of the adult bodies that surrounded me. There was nowhere to look as people towered around me. The only security lay in the hand of my father who stood beside me. Mumblings and the faint shuffling of feet added to the strangeness of the situation. Then, at one stage, I looked at my father in bewilderment as he plunged down onto one knee and in a few short moments he popped up again.

This was my one of my earliest memory of what I now know to be Mass. The crowd that I was 'squashed into' at that young age was the weekly Sunday congregation in the parish that was to be home to my family for many years to follow. The personality of the priest didn't matter, nor even the direction the altar faced. I've no memory whether the Mass was in Latin or English. I just remember my father plunging to his knee at a point in the Mass called the consecration. I asked him what was he doing and he just said, very gently, 'sssssshhhhh'. This moment never left me and his whole demeanour was somehow captured in the words of John the Baptist, 'There is one greater than me here'.

When I see people walk around churches today; even going up for readings at funerals or weddings there is little awareness of the need to bow, genuflect or pause. Somehow this reflects one of the errors of our days which could be summed up in the words 'there is no one greater than me here'.

Gazing at the crib scene one notices those who rest on one or both knees. To grow in our spiritual lives have to move beyond a God whose duty it is only to provide for our satisfactions and our desires. At times organised religions peddle union with God as something up for sale in the magazine rack in the church or even the local supermarket. To kneel or bow down is to let go of our manipulation of God for our own ends and simply to trust in his goodness and bow to the excitement of mystery. Even at a psychological level this is a great perspective because if we set our hopes on vain things then we are sure to experience despair and God knows ... there is enough of that 'd' word around.

'If we were incapable of humility we would be incapable of joy, because humility alone can destroy the self-centredness that makes joy impossible.'

Thomas Merton

• • • • • • • • • •

New Seeds of Contemplation, (London: Burns and Oates, 2002), p. 124.

#not_christian

Sometimes it is hard to imagine that those who witnessed the birth of Jesus were not Christian. They hadn't been to Mass, hadn't recited the third joyful mystery of the rosary, the nativity or hadn't even paid their Christmas Dues!

Whatever content there is in every faith tradition or world religion there is always the space for mystery, contemplation and silence. Cultures make room for inward and outward expressions of faith in varying degrees, but they change to accommodate the times and traditions of the people at particular points in time. The wise men followed their star and brought gifts as was the custom in their place of origin, but little is told of what they said but that they bowed down and worshipped. The shepherds on the other hand went home 'singing praises to their God' (Lk 2:20).

God inhabits a culture and his presence is mediated through this same culture. It is where humanity meets God. No one is excluded from this hope be they shepherds, wise men, astronauts, teachers, hairdressers or farmers. Sometimes a culture is laden down with religious symbols and preferences and at other times the religious content of a culture is more difficult to identify. This is more and more the case in Western civilisation where the name Christmas abounds, but the religious content of this festival is put in a mincer and extracted for all sorts of politically correct and incorrect reasons.

It's time to follow the example of the wise men and shepherds and discover the divine content where it is to be found and honour it; even sing aloud about it on the way home from where ever we find it. Once found, a culture can be remoulded to accommodate any amount of religious content, allowing it to grow like a spring bulb in fresh soil.

> *'In the end, there can be no surprise*
> *— nor surely is there any contradiction –*
> *that people can embrace the blessings of*
> *modern life, even reach hungrily for more*
> *of them, yet know they've lost something*
> *in the bargain, and grieve for it.'*

Robert Kanigel

• • • • • • • • •

On an Irish Island, (New York: Random House, 2012), p. 254.

50

HE DAY AND NOT THE NIGHT AR

#poverty

Poverty has used up a lot of ink. Books, documents, policies and many other documents fill the shelves of libraries as they try to dissect the causes and remedy the effects of its presence in societies and families.

I was standing at a bus stop one day. One of those east winds was blowing – the type that'd cut through you. An elderly lady huddled in the corner of the shelter trying to escape the winds sharp piercings. She was doing her best but the shelter stood six inches off the ground and the wind was doing terrible damage to her feet and ankles. We nodded to one another and I buried myself in my scarf.

I can't remember the exact reason, whether it was a storm, floods or an industrial dispute but the buses stopped running. Trying to offer consolation I said, 'sure we can always get a taxi'. I knew immediately from the way she looked at me that this was not an option. I asked her where she lived and I said 'I'm passing that way'. When I eventually hailed a taxi she hopped in. We put her shopping in the boot. I told the taxi driver where I was heading to but that we'd be stopping at this lady's home on the way. She didn't say much as she listened to the taxi driver and myself chatting about the woes of the world.

When we got to her destination she thanked me and said she'd say a prayer for me and my family. It was along walk for her without transport; especially in that cold. I told the taxi driver to turn back from the direction we came from to drop me home. I explained what had happened. He switched the meter off for the rest of the journey. We talked differently then. For a lot of the short journey we talked about our blessings. This was in contrast to our conversation when the lady was in the taxi when both of us were trying to outdo one another as each of us moaned about life, cyclists and politicians and indeed everything else that we could think of.

When we got to my destination we sat for a while and chatted. I gave him the fare; what was on the meter and a few bob more. I stepped out of the car and felt the cold again. As I walked up to my door I stopped for a moment and saw the old lady's face before my eyes. In that moment I realised what poverty is. I've read about it, even taught it and discussed it in various settings, but in that moment I realised that poverty is simply not having a choice. The person I see sleeping in a doorway has no choice; the one who

steps into a boat in the Mediterranean often has no choice; the old lady for whom there is no bus has no choice. If I am afforded the luxury of a choice about my mode of transport, what I eat, where I go for a drink I'm a wealthy person.

There are many today who have no choice, many who can see a future that will steal their choices and there are many in the past who had little or no choice. We remember one great example at this time of the year; 'She wrapped him in swaddling clothes and laid him in a manger, because there was no room for them in the inn' (Lk 2:7).

> *'What is in our collective long term interest does not necessarily match the short-term domestic interests of politicians or all their constituencies.'*
>
> Ian Goldin, Geoffrey Cameron and Meera Balarajan
>
> • • • • • • • • • •
>
> *Exceptional People: How Migration Shaped Our World and Will Define Our Future,*
> (New Jersey: Princeton University Press, 2011).

#protector

It's hard to know when someone becomes an adult these days … ask any parent who has children in college. So let us speculate; when does someone become an adult? When they reach eighteen, twenty-one or when they graduate? Is it when they learn to drive, or when they move out of home or even when they get their first job? Your guess is as good as mine!

I listened to one Australian aboriginal give an account as to when the children in his village become adults. The boy is entrusted to the elders who share stories of the tribe. These stories relate to survival. Stories, song and dance relay information letting the candidate know he can find food, water and other essentials. They are told what and how to kill and what to respect. The dignity of their people is upheld in the way they remember those gone before them and who remain with them in the present moment. Their culture unapologetically believes that we are connected in a deeply spiritual way with those gone before us.

But let's get back to the point. When the young boy returns to the village he is deemed to be an adult as the people of the village now know that he will stand between the village and danger in order to protect those in it.

The Nativity narratives of the Gospel tell us that Joseph sensed danger and he stood between that danger and those he loved.

`It is no surprise that the first and always unwelcome message of male initiation rites is LIFE – IS – HARD.'

Richard Rohr

. . . .

Falling Upward: A Spirituality for the Two Halves of Life,
(San Francisco: Jossey Bass Publishers, 2011).

#saviour

I lived in Bondi parish for a while and every morning I'd go for a walk on the beach. I have to admit I never saw a rescue taking place – maybe I unconsciously avoided the rush hour! There was a story that did the rounds while I was there. It describes a rather frantic lady running up to the surf rescue team and in an obviously traumatised state screamed, 'Help, help, my son *the architect*, is drowning'. She placed more emphasis on his occupation rather than his plight! It's funny how one small aspect of self can take over and take on more importance than it deserves.

I remember on another occasion visiting a lady whose husband had died. I knew she bore the cross of a rather tough marriage and the relationship was complicated by his alcoholism. They had no children and the neighbours had gathered. As is customary I asked was there anything that she would like me to say about her late husband at his funeral. There was an uncomfortable silence as she dug deep to think of something in response to my question. I'll never forget it, 'He never left me short father'.

What she was saying was that he put the agreed housekeeping money on the table – not a penny more nor a penny less. She couldn't find much more to say about him. There was no other romantic or nostalgic tit-bit to offer – just that crumb of basic provision. That was all he meant to her after many years of marriage or even cohabitation.

The sadness of life is that it can remain unlived, not fully understood or even limited in its realisations. The name given to the child who we remember at Christmas was Jesus. Translated it means 'saviour'. In reality the saving act has evolved into the act of saving us from our sinfulness … that's the job that we've reduced him to in many religious circles.

There are many occasions in the Gospels when Jesus tells

someone that their sins are forgiven but he does much more. His ministry cannot be reduced to forgiveness alone. Most of his engagements and stories help people to live well, even to flourish. We reduced our 'saviour' to a life guard who rescues us when we get into bother rather than someone who wants to teach us to swim in the waters of life, so that we can enjoy that life to the full. Reducing his role to a mere forgiver of sins undermines the scope of the relationship we can have with him.

> *'When a child is born, its parents immediately begin to talk to it. Long before it can understand, a child is fed with words. The mother and father do not talk to the child so as to communicate information. They are talking it into life ... Slowly it will be able to find a place in the love that its parents share.'*

Timothy Radcliffe

. . . .

Sing a New Song, (Dublin: Dominican Publications, 1999), p. 152.

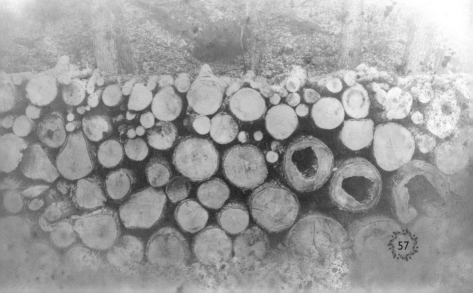

#spiritual_or_religious

The terms spiritual and religious are often used interchangeably and most often when people identify themselves as 'spiritual but not religious'. Joseph and Mary, as they are depicted in the

Christmas Story in Matthew's Gospel, appear deeply spiritual. They use inner resources to overcome difficulties; these difficulties and challenges don't have to be spelt out to us who are familiar with the account of the birth of Jesus. These inner resources open them to occasions when God's promptings and grace help nudge them into a safer place, even though at times comfort might tempt them to sit still for a while.

The narrative in the Gospel of Matthew, however, shows how deeply they are immersed in the religion of their days. Quotes from the Old Testament show how these moments are part of something greater and of which they are an important part. The two, religion and spirituality, are one. One definition of spirituality that I cannot forget is that it is the art of making connections. In our prayers and in our ponderings we try to connect with someone or something that can help us make our paths straight and find our own 'Immanuel' or God who is with us (Mt 1:23). If we remain solely spiritual (if that can be done) then we are left with nothing to connect to, good religion helps us to connect deeply through its rituals, peoples, wisdom and traditions.

'In Jesus, God took on human flesh. The spirit of God overshadowed Mary, and in her all enmity between spirit and body was overcome. Thus God's Spirit was united with the human spirit, and the human body became the temple destined to be lifted up into the intimacy of God through resurrection.'

Henri J. M. Nouwen

- - - - - - - - -

The Inner Voice of Love, (London; Darton, Longman and Todd, 1997), p. 17.

#taking_hold_of_the_season

The dawn chorus woke me every morning and the sunset eased me into a night of peaceful slumber. This was daily life in the outback of the Northern Territories in Australia. No electricity, no running water, no bells, clocks or wi-fi; nothing artificial to dictate the daily order and so nature took over. I knew I was on holidays, but it was extraordinarily relaxing to enter a rhythm of life without the thousands of rhythms that compete for attention in what we call the 'real' world.

Eric Smith declared the twenty-first century as the century of the 'attention economy' where global corporations would compete to maximise the number of 'eyeballs' they could engage and control. Ironically we, the subject, because we want to avoid the fearful state of monotony, buy into the game; allowing our eyeballs to be stolen and abused every second and every fraction of a second. This is particularly true of the seasons we refer to as Advent and Christmas when commercialism is running at break-neck speed and our eyeballs are popping out of our head.

One sociologist said that the only way for humanity to survive the excesses of the twenty-first century is the cultivation of habits. Habits are times set aside to do certain things to the exclusion of other things in the belief that the outcome of the habit or habits are beneficial to us. Rather than allowing our eyeballs to be caught in the commercial headlights why not develop habits that allow our eyeballs to rest on things that restore us? Why not be in control of your eyeballs for a period of time? Once a week look to the stars or even get up that little bit early to watch a sunrise, which even in winter can be stunning. Maybe have an 'own your eyeball day'. I don't want to be too prescriptive – I'm sure you get the idea ... eyeball to eyeball like!

'Because of the infinity of content accessible 24/7, there will always be something online more informative, surprising, funny, diverting, impressive than anything in one's immediate actual circumstances.'

Jonathan Crary

· · · · · · · · · ·

24/7, (London: Verso Books, 2014), p. 59.

#talk_is_cheap

This Christmas season is a time when we hear the phrase that the 'word became flesh'. This refers to God becoming one of us but it brings us a real and timely challenge. Many who profess the name of Christian live in ideas workshops – the challenge is to put flesh on Christian ideas and ideals. The Word became flesh as the Son of God, but the word of life needs to take flesh constantly through our actions. This season reminds us we are part of a divine intention, not a world of empty words or attractive ideas that we can admire like a shop window display. As my mother often said to me 'talk is cheap son'.

'God beyond all understanding bringing balance and harmony to the boundless resources, powerful energies, stores of strength, endless potential of our being.'

Sr Stan

• • • • • • • • •

Awakening Inner Peace, (Dublin: Columba Books, 2018), p. 181.

#tangmalangmaloo

An Irish priest who took the pen-name John O'Brien wrote poems depicting out-back life in Australia. His name in real life was Patrick Joseph Hartigan and he was the son of Irish emigrants from Lisseycasey, County Clare. His first book was published in 1921 and has become an Australian epic. Entitled, *Around the Boree Log and Other Verses,* it relates stories of weather, hardship, character, flood and flower. Far outside the cities of Sydney and Melbourne there is a beauty in places like Yass, Goulbourn and Narrendara. He captured the magic of these rural areas in poetic verse. Like most poets he gives insight into the lived experience of people and his work is a fine social history.

His poem entitled 'Tangmalangmaloo' recounts the visit of the bishop to the local school to examine the students on their understanding of the Catechism which was basically a question and answer session to see if the students could progress towards the sacraments. One might be correct in assuming that this story was based in reality because Fr Hartigan, as he was known, spent many of his years visiting schools as an inspector. However he rather dolefully admits in the poem that, 'Christian knowledge wilts, alas, at Tangmalangmaloo'.

The poem creates a dynamic tension between the pomposity of the bishop and the utter ignorant innocence of one country lad who was squeezed tightly into a bench. He is described as an 'overgrown two-storey lad' whom the bishop decides to examine. In fairness he threw him an easy ball asking 'why is Christmas Day the greatest day of the year?' To the shock of everyone the two-storey lad reacted with an enthusiasm that was normally saved for break time and the final bell. His bigness and awkwardness meant that desks fell over and 'vases on the shelf [went] askew' as he jumped up from his seat with eagerness to respond to his lordship.

The answer the boy from Tangmalangmaloo gave is best relayed in its original form;

The ready answer bared a fact no Bishop ever knew –
It's the day before the races out at Tangmalangmaloo.

Christmas day can mean many things for many people! What is Christmas Day for you?

> *'Because of their isolation, the sisters would not have available to them many of the traditional practices of conventual piety, such as daily Mass. Like bush carpenters, then, they would have to knock together a rough-and-ready spirituality from whatever materials were at hand.'*

Edmund Campion

· · · · · · · · ·

Australian Catholics, (Victoria: Viking, 1987), p. 49.

This extract describes the early life and work of the Josephite Sisters who were set up by Mary McKillop to serve the needs of Australians. She was canonised as Australia's first saint on the 17 October 2010.

#the_committee

Someone I knew compared a committee to a dark alley that slowly lured a good idea into its darkest corner and mugged it to death! We've all sat on committees where the great undone remains as the great undone. You go around the table and people utter what should be happening and somebody should do this, that, or the other. The great silence descends when the chair asks 'now who will take responsibility for this, or that or the other?'… The good ideas don't make it out alive.

It's a good job that a committee wasn't charged with the idea of sending Jesus among us … we'd still be in the wilderness looking for salvation! Luckily, there is room for the undemocratic and impulsive action of a loving Father.

`The old allegedly patented ways of tackling life's challenges don't work anymore, while new and effective ones are nowhere in sight or in abominably short supply.'

Zygmunt Bauman and Carlo Bordoni

• • • • • • • • • •

State of Crisis, (Cambridge: Polity Press, 2014), p. 24

#the_'lectric

Driving home one evening I was enthralled by a radio documentary that related recordings of the last place in Ireland to receive electricity or the 'lectric' as it was called in the local dialect. The location was aptly called 'The Black Valley', and is in County Kerry.

The producers went ahead of the installation and interviewed people who were full of frightened expectation as the cables made their way closer and closer to the last door in the country to receive this new form of power. An elderly couple were the last house on the road and being a proud home owner all she was worried about was having a clean house to welcome their new guest that promised to transform their lives. As the presenter talked you could hear her scrubbing, moving, washing and replacing over and over again. The familiar sound of a tin pail full of water and a mop slushing around a stone floor only served to increase the sense of excited anticipation.

When the 'lectric' was eventually installed the switch in the house was flicked and lo and behold despite all the cleaning and polishing the brazen 'lectric' bulb revealed dirt, cobwebs and dust in places they didn't even know existed in their humble abode. There was utter embarrassment and discomfort all round.

We don't see light but light helps us see. The opening of St John's Gospel is called the prologue and it tells us that Jesus is the 'light that shines in the darkness and the darkness has not overcome it'. He is described as 'the light' as his ways, insights and teachings help us to see the world and our existence in a refreshingly unlimited manner. Sometimes his light, like the 'lectric', may also show us where we have to tidy up our lives!

'To talk you need to be able to dismantle defensive walls, open the door of the house and offer human kindness.'

Bergoli and Skórka, 'On Heaven and Earth'

. . . .

In Zygmunt Bauman and Stanislaw Obirek, *On the World and Ourselves*, (Cambridge: Polity Press, 2015), p. 20.

#the_visit

It seems like years ago now but there were times when the thing to do was to visit people in hospital when they had their newborn baby. Rooms and wards would be full of flowers and cards that were laden with congratulatory messages.

However, things have changed. With increasing security fears, risk of infection and privacy rights it nearly easier to do a prison visit than get into a maternity hospital! One of my fondest memories is not being looked at when spoken to in maternity hospitals.

Besotted and distracted by the beautiful new baby both parents spoke to me while watching their child — totally mesmerised and totally understandable.

I was drawn back to these moments when I read how St Teresa of Ávila described prayer — 'Prayer is God looking at us lovingly'. Forget the words just sit back for a few moments and see God looking lovingly upon you. If you find it difficult just sit in front of a crib for a few moments and see those parents looking lovingly on their child despite their rather precarious situation.

'He looks upon His servant in her lowliness,
henceforth all ages will call me blessed.'

Mary's Magnificat (Lk 1:46–55)

• • • • • • • • •

#tribal

He was every inch of what you'd expect a wise man to be. Tall, ponderous, intuitive and generous with those who weren't wasting his time. His professional life was lived as a professor of sociology and a priest. He lived through the horrors of the Rwandan Genocide, and he lives through it still as he endeavours to reason with the tremendous evils he witnessed. I can still hear the quiver in his voice when twenty years after the genocide he said 'you know that humanity has crossed a line when fathers can murder their own children'. In truth he saw the slaughter of many innocents. He paused and said nothing for quite a while.

A few weeks later I was reading up on the genocide. The author, another priest said that 'tribal identities became more important than baptismal identity'. Either we are all the same as children of God and we demand to both give and receive mutual respect, or we create tribes where we make ourselves more important or more valuable than others who occupy the same space.

'The most important lesson we can learn from
the social and political instability
of other nations today ... is that the
institutional foundations of ethnic harmony
are fragile and need to be continuously
nurtured and reaffirmed.'

Tamar Jacoby

. . . .

Reinventing the Melting Pot: The New immigrants and What it Means to be American,
(New York: Basic Books, 2004), p. 99.

#uileann_pipes

I just love the uileann pipes. Whether they are being played to plunge the depths of a slow air or blended with numerous other instruments I am enraptured. In a session I seek them out with my ear to hear their unique contribution in the midst of all the other instruments. The chanter and the drones of the pipes create a space where one can sit and be enriched by the nuances between the notes and chords.

My favourite story about the pipes is one that was told to me by John Sheahan of *The Dubliners* at the thirtieth anniversary Mass for Matt Kiernan who was a legendary uileann pipe maker. John's father and Matt were both Gardaí and were based in different stations in Dublin. Matt was a great pipe maker but parts for the pipes were both expensive and hard to come by. John told me that there was hardly a Garda baton to be found in the stations they worked in as they were frequently 'requisitioned' to be transformed into chanters for the pipes that Matt was working on. The ebony timber of the baton was a perfect raw material for the chanter.

When I listen to the pipes I often compare the notes to our good selves, each note is a moment when we can dance to the tune of the Almighty. The drones and regulators bring us into touch with something deeper which I see as the mystery of God swirling around us and supporting our human efforts as we try to rise above that which can drag us down.

> 'For centuries philosophers and scientists argued over the existence of God, as if it were a matter of speculation or hypothesis that could be proved or disproved ... To hear God we have to learn to listen, and to listen we need to create a kind of silence in our soul.'
>
> Jonathan Sacks

. . . .

Faith in the Future, (London: Darton, Longman, Todd Ltd., 1995) p. 136.

Thanks John for giving me permission to share this story

70

#wrapping_up_God

Putting God into Christmas wrapping can limit his presence and narrow his role in our lives. We take the wrapping on and off as it suits us or as we need his presence but always on our terms. When something happens us, particularly if something goes horribly wrong we may get upset with him.

If I was God I'd feel used and abused. Creating a God that comes and goes as we need him is not the God that led the Wise Men to the stable or the one that spoke to Joseph. Theirs was a God that both guided them and journeyed with them through obstacles, adventures and crises. Theirs was a God they could have said no to, but they believed in faithfulness to a journey and a dream, and they believed that faithfulness was mutual not one-sided. They believed that everything emanates from him and everything goes back to him and we are part of that coming and going.

The God of the wrapping is one who depends on us to let him in and out of life, whereas seeing him as the ground of everything gives God a chance to be God. For instance when you step into prison cell is God present? The wrapping model might say he's not because of the crime or the person in the cell whom you meet. In those awful family conflicts can we hold onto the belief that if we are faithful to what is right and good that things will work out or do we succumb to petty jealousies and age-old disputes? Believing that God is omnipresent means having the hope of the wise men and the courage of Joseph, which means believing that he will be faithful to us even when he appears to abandon us.

When Mary went to her cousin Elizabeth she'd didn't sound as if her God had let her down though in human terms she was in a right pickle. Despite being with child in a difficult situation she simply said 'the Almighty does great things for me' and God's presence did unfold mightily in her life and in the lives of many generations.

> *'Even when someone's life appears completely wrecked, even when we see it devastated by vices or addictions, God is present there.'*
>
> Pope Francis
>
> • • • • • • • • •
>
> *Gaudete et Exsultate*, para. 42.